Sincerely,

Singleness

Sincerely, Singleness

JOSHUA ERICKSON

TLB

To the Church
To the Married
To the Single
To All

CONTENTS

1

To Whom I am Concerned With,

I would like to hit the ground running and begin with a mental exercise. I want you to imagine yourself in a church. You are sitting in a wooden pew, a metal folding chair, or whatever form you would like your seat to take. You are among a crowd—your choice of how large or small. From the platform, the following question is presented to the crowd "How many of you are single?"

Next, you will likely find a collection of hands raised in response, with definite hesitation accompanying each raised hand. I venture to say this is not only a mental exercise but something that you have experienced yourself. Either as one of the individuals with a solitary hand raised or among the crowd—a witness to all the people who identify with this group. The infamous group: single people in the church.

Singleness by nature is foreign to no one. All have been there, some longer than others and some still there, but singleness is a topic that includes everyone none the less. The discussion of singleness, in or out of the church, sparks a range of different emotions, opinions, and stories. But within the church, it can certainly be a unique experience. Singleness within the church includes the addition of scriptures, ideas on how relationships and God's will work together, and a dusty collection of cliché sayings with seemingly no expiration date.

Next, I would like to ask you to tweak the previous mental exercise just a bit. Let us go back in history, narrowing it down to around two thousand or so odd years ago. You now find yourself sitting in an unknown temple in Jerusalem with the same question posed to a new crowd. From the crowd's response, you would find the hand raised of a young man roughly in his late twenties. To simply name drop, you would find Jesus of Nazareth with a raised hand identifying with this exact classification—single.

Now, it is common church knowledge that Jesus was single in His thirty and some odd years here on the earth. Yet, with this fact in mind, I struggle to remember if I have ever heard the topic of singleness discussed with a positive connection to the life of Jesus.

The various aspects of how Jesus walked on this earth are highly respected and admired as we aspire to be more like Christ, with the exclusion of His singleness. All the while, the topic of singleness exists in the church with more questions than answers. And these unanswered questions are partnered with a growing frustration and confusion that surround the topic of how to live as a single person within the church.

While the connection between Jesus and singleness is still discussed, this discussion is often used in an attempt to lessen the sadness of being single. A sadness that is often accompanied by feelings of loneliness and emptiness toward missing out on the joys of marriage. And while the joys of marriage should be celebrated in their entirety, I fear that we are choosing to use the connection between Jesus and singleness as a temporary fix for issues we do not seek to handle or understand, and instead, only seek to find the appearance of a solution to avoid dealing with the situation altogether.

My main concern is not with the methods that are used in trying to help those who are single, but with the lack of urgency to change these methods when faced with the unsettling truth that healthy singleness is far from a reality. And I fear that the continuation of these ineffective methods may only be done in hopes of buying enough time for the situation to resolve itself, instead of in seeking out an actual resolution.

To seek out a resolution needed for the church who was brought into existence by Jesus. One who only ever identified with this relationship status alone. A resolution that is needed for the existence of the frustration and confusion that exists in the church surrounding singleness.

I write all that follows with a hope of moving toward a culture where both those who are single and those who are married can find equal joy and contentment in walking out their faith with God. This hope has been spurred on by spending the entirety of my twenties seeking God's will for my life. While also seeking to grow in the understanding of how to pursue a Godly spouse along that very path and identifying as a single person for much of that time.

Along this path, I have found that I have learned more about singleness than I have ever longed to find. And in getting far more than I bargained for, God has laid it on my heart to share what He has shown and taught me along the way, as is most often the case when God teaches us something. This journey has brought me through many different situations and seasons of singleness: the season of becoming the right person, the season of not seeking a spouse, the season of giving people a chance, the season of pondering maybe I am too picky, and lastly, the season of just completely trusting God and doing what He has placed in front of me. And one of the things that I have learned is that the idea of seasons can be a very dangerous thing.

But even with many lessons learned through these experiences, I write on this subject with great caution. Writing with an awareness of trying to avoid using my own frustrations or personal feelings as a foundation, but rather seeking to bring into proper light what the Bible teaches in combination with what God has taught me. It would be simple to write in a way that makes this subject easy to digest. Writing with the misleading of personal frustrations and feelings that would only give us momentary peace in the end.

Rather, the pursuit is to seek out a trustworthy and lasting biblical peace on the subject, which is likely to find itself in a less appetizing form. Furthermore, I would be inclined to avoid writing on this topic entirely, with a motivation of wanting to escape the topic's complicated and puzzling nature. While in all honesty, hesitating most of all to avoid being known as the "one who wrote that book on singleness."

This hesitation is found because the topic of singleness does not find itself in the same field of respect as a relationship topic such as marriage—with marriage experts often being held in a place of great respect. I believe this is a result of viewing singleness as a temporary path, only to be endured instead of to be lived out. And in turn, the value of singleness is then diminished when facing a comparison to marriage. And it is because of the concerns of these realizations that I find a great urgency to write about singleness.

I am concerned that we have created a culture in the church where singleness cannot thrive, and that we now face the alarming reality that singleness in our current culture may barely be able to survive. The existence of this unhealthy culture often succeeds in hindering singleness from being used as God intends it to be—if it be for a part of a person's life or the whole of it.

The following chapters are certainly for all to read, but I address this specifically to the church—the body of Christ. Written equally to both those who are single and to those who are married. Words written for the whole body of Christ. With the desire to see the entire body made whole. The body of Christ, with the one at its head who walked the earth solely as a single person, yet whose lessons we value in no less of a way because of His singleness.

Please take the following chapters to heart, as I believe they will not only help to bring those who associate with singleness in closer connection to the body of Christ but will also help those who no longer associate with singleness to better understand those who do.

Now for those who are single, I would like to state that I do not intend to help ease the pain of singleness or attempt to put words on paper as a bandage for a wound. But instead, I long to see the wound we have covered up begin to heal—a wound that I fear may already be infected to begin with. And to be able to finally face this hidden wound, one that is often picked at in broken solitude. With an aim toward finding clarity on how God intends to use singleness in its healthy and functional form.

The areas that I have picked to discuss are ones that God has stirred within me to bring to the table of conversation; areas which I believe hold an overdue need for urgent attention. To bring to attention in hopes of moving toward a healthy view of singleness for all within the church. And motivated by a heart to neither fight for nor defend a particular relationship status, single or married, but only to see both used by God as He intends.

Let us aim to see the body of Christ thriving and the frustration and sadness of singleness lessened. Where the pursuit of finding marriage within the will of God does not overshadow the very will of God itself. And seeing Christians, whether single or married, holding their relationship with God as the most important relationship status of them all.

Sincerely,
Singleness

2

The Truth:

Singleness, Marriage, and The Bible

Let us begin the discussion by searching for what the Bible teaches regarding singleness and marriage. With this being the only place to start if we desire to find life-giving direction and instruction on these topics, instead of only momentary peace and relief.

The topics of both singleness and marriage can quickly become dangerous without the Bible as the foundation for the perspectives and beliefs that surround each relationship status. Without the proper foundation, we start down a path guided by emotional beliefs and personal experiences, only to eventually find ourselves more confused and frustrated. But in starting with God's truth, we build upon a solid and lasting foundation, and a foundation that is suited for all to build upon.

Yet, even with a biblical starting point, there are still many tough questions that must be faced. Questions, such as, what does the Bible say about singleness and marriage? Is it better to be single or married? What should a person pursue and how? Let us go to the Bible to see what it says about singleness, marriage, and where to start in seeking out answers to these tough questions.

Singleness	Marriage
Now to the unmarried and the widows I say: It is good for them to stay unmarried, as I am. (1 Corinthians 7:8 NIV)	The LORD God said, "It is not good for the man to be alone. I will make a helper suitable for him." (Genesis 2:18 NIV)
But if he has decided firmly not to marry and there is no urgency and he can control his passion, he does well not to marry. (1 Corinthians 7:37 NLT)	He who finds a wife finds what is good, and receives favor from the LORD. (Proverbs 18:22 NIV)

Note: I encourage the entire reading of 1 Corinthians 7, as it is an extremely valuable chapter in regard to the overall discussion of relationships.

After reading these verses, what do they mean for an individual and the relationship status they may associate with? The first thing that scripture shows us is that both singleness and marriage are good in nature. Meaning that both are positive and beneficial, even if both are difficult and include a wide range of hardships that may be encountered.

Now, if God has intended both relationship statuses for good, then neither one should be known as inherently sad or something to be endured. These distorted views form out of a misinterpretation of how the original intention of each relationship status is seen. If we find this to be the experience or view for either one, then it is not the relationship or lack of one that is the issue but the handling of each relationship status and what we believe the meaning for each one to be.

Oftentimes, in life, we are asked to pick sides on a topic, but concerning the topic of relationships, this can be a dangerous thing to do.

In 1 Corinthians 7:35, Paul speaks about relationships very clearly and shows us what is most important in regard to a relationship status, and it is far from the status of single or married.

> I am saying this for your benefit, not to place
> restrictions on you. I want you to do whatever
> will help you serve the Lord best, with as few
> distractions as possible.
> (1 Corinthians 7:35 NLT)

At the core of this verse is a truth that is too often overlooked when discussing the topic of relationships. A truth declaring that there is only one relationship status that holds a priority over any other, a relationship with God Himself. All other relationships show themselves to be secondary in nature. The truth about singleness and marriage is that the Bible prioritizes a relationship with God over both.

The Bible is both pro-singleness and pro-marriage, but it supersedes taking a stance for either relationship status over the other by holding the pursuit of a relationship with God above all other things.

The previous verses regarding singleness and marriage may seem to contradict each other, but the context for each verse must not be forgotten. The verses regarding marriage show the necessity and intended blessing of human relationships, in addition to our relationship with God. While the verses regarding singleness show the importance of keeping a right relationship with God the priority over any human relationship.

Adam needed human relationships in addition to his relationship with God, as we all do, but human relationships were never meant to supplant the supreme importance of our relationship with God.

> **The truth about singleness and marriage is that the Bible prioritizes a relationship with God over both.**

A Reminder For All

In trying to figure out if a specific relationship status is better than the other, there is no way to determine if either being single or married holds a greater place in a person's walk with God, and because of this, I am very thankful. For I believe the will of God is far more profound than holding such a vital importance on a relationship status, a status which often finds itself out of a person's control.

Now, this by no means is meant to belittle the nature and importance of relationships. But rather to make sure it is possible for a person to be confident in checking whichever relationship box they find themselves identifying with and to know that a relationship status does not halt God's plan for their life. A plan that is meant to produce a righteous and steadfast faith, becoming more like Christ, and glorifying Him with one's life along every step of the way. This relationship with God must be the main focus as one grows to become more like Christ, instead of having a focus on a certain relationship status.

As a person pursues a deeper relationship with God and the plans He has for them, they often need to walk this path out with increasingly greater steps of faith as God reveals only a few of the upcoming steps at a time. In this, one must have the flexibility to walk out the journey of any relationship status—even if they find themselves asking the question "why" more than they would like to admit. The plan that God has for each person is quite unique and extremely hard to decipher. And Proverbs 20:24 gives us great wisdom regarding how to handle the uncertainty of our path:

> The LORD directs our steps, so why try to
> understand everything along the way?
> (Proverbs 20:24 NLT)

Now, if both singleness and marriage are good in nature and the will of God is not something a person can fully understand, then why do these two statuses seem to silently wage war against each other within the church?

For a single person in church desiring to marry, there is an ever-growing sadness if the pursuit of marriage is prolonged. Bringing with it many frustrations, no path forward, and only a few short-term pursuits in attempts of distraction. This situation is often greater magnified by the view of singleness as nothing more than the step that comes before marriage and often coupled with a common view of the need for further growth and an increased pursuit of God before qualifying to move forward.

Yet, singleness is not meant to be a step in life. For we are always single in nature. And a person still holds their own unique and individual identity regardless of their relationship status. The contrast that is found between singleness and marriage is rooted in the covenant decision of marriage.

At the crux of marriage is a choice. A decision that holds the deepest level of commitment and sacrifice. Yet, a person who chooses to marry is still one person, but instead now focusing on putting another person's needs before their own. Within the powerful covenant of a God-centered marriage, a glimpse of God's perfect love for us can be shown through imperfect people, and His heavenly love is expedited down to earth.

Even though marriage can be a beautiful portrait used in highlighting God's love, this does not mean singleness cannot. Through marriage, we are able to see a representation of how God chooses to love us, yet Jesus showed that this is possible through singleness as well.

We may not choose to highlight the singleness of Jesus and the fact that He performed His ministry solely as a single person. Yet, the singleness that He walked out did not hinder Him from showing the most compassionate and sacrificial love to those He encountered. Jesus's singleness is something that we have seemingly disconnected from His story, but His singleness, most importantly, reminds us that He had a purpose on earth that went beyond a temporary relationship status. His priority was always to keep His relationship with the Father above all other things here on earth.

Jesus constantly reminded others that He only did what the Father told Him. And it was His relationship with the Father that influenced how He dealt with people. Even though He had close and intimate human relationships, in dealing with people, He always showed that His relationship with the Father was of the highest importance. This is a simple reminder from the life of Jesus about where our relationship priority should always find itself placed.

Next Stop?

Marriage is indeed a sacred relationship ordained by God and a great relationship pursuit in life. However, it is not the greatest pursuit in life. The desire or pursuit of marriage must never find itself in contest with the pursuit of God. And single people can certainly find themselves waiting at a stop along their journey in walking with God, expectantly hoping to find someone to join them on their travels before they move on. And many married people may also choose to "arrive" at marriage and get off a few stops too soon on the path that God has intended them to travel on.

Both the single person and the married person may find themselves in a different place but doing the same thing in principle, failing to pursue God's plans and more of God Himself. With this being a very devastating decision to make for a person's faith. And this stopping short of seeking God applies not only to the category of relationship pursuits but to any area in life that may be potentially idolized. This can lead to the blessing that God has intended to give a person, quickly becoming the very thing that stops them from moving along the path that it was found upon.

We may know the truth that God wants to bless us with more than we can imagine, yet we may still choose to stop, sit, and wait for one specific blessing, all the while God is pleading for us to keep seeking Him with all our heart and to continue pushing forward on the path He has placed before us. For this is where we find more than just blessings from God but also His purpose for our lives. And this is only found in seeking His will and more of Him.

> Delight yourself in the LORD and he will give
> you the desires of your heart.
> (Psalm 37:4 NIV)

This stopping short can be an obvious thing in a person's life, but it may often find itself to be more of a subtle change. A change that is only noticed by those in close relationship with a person. Someone close enough to the person to know what God has already spoken to them. It may seem that the person has not changed at all and is still seeking God. They may still be going to church and living their life as usual, but as humans, we are unable to see what may have changed in their heart. The truth of this change lies with answering a question that only the person themselves can honestly answer: Are they still pursuing God as they should be? Oftentimes, a person already knows the answer to this question, but they continue on in silence, seeking to avoid ever answering it. Ultimately avoiding the action of change that is required with an honest answered.

Purpose Instead of Problems

In scripture, we see that Jesus walked the earth just as every human finds themselves walking. He faced the same problems and pain that we face while seeking to do the will of God. But it is simply forgotten that He also found himself walking out a life of singleness on His way to the cross. But even with this stated, I fear a common view in church culture is to view a single person as falling just short of the mark. Seen as a person who is missing something that may be keeping them from reaching their full potential. Yet with Jesus, His singleness was never a hindrance to His calling. And if we find ourselves overemphasizing the singleness of an individual, we position ourselves to miss out on the important details and purpose surrounding a person's relationship with God. And with single people, this detailed focus on a relationship status has not gone unnoticed.

As a single person seeks to grow in relationship with God and in greater connection with the church body, they are often reminded of the lack of a spouse in their life. The encouragement and support of Godly marriages should be strongly present in the church, yet with the lack of promoting a Godly singleness apart from it leading to marriage, we are not promoting Godly singleness at all. Without the coexistence of support for Godly singleness alongside the support for Godly marriage, we are creating a dead-end destination for single people, with no direction to face but toward marriage.

As a person seeks to grow in a deeper relationship with God, singleness becomes more of an obvious label if one desires to serve in the church. Single people are aware they are missing the valuable companion by their side to complete what is sometimes seen as their "ministry potential" puzzle, and marriage can even become a qualification for those seeking certain ministry opportunities. Yet, Paul writes in 1 Corinthians 7:32-34 of a differing perspective on relationships and their role in a person's ministry potential.

> [32] I want you to be free from the concerns of this life. An unmarried man can spend his time doing the Lord's work and thinking how to please him. [33] But a married man has to think about his earthly responsibilities and how to please his wife. [34] His interests are divided. In the

same way, a woman who is no longer married or has never been married can be devoted to the Lord and holy in body and in spirit. But a married woman has to think about her earthly responsibilities and how to please her husband.
(1 Corinthians 7:32-34 NLT)

There is certainly great value in having a person at one's side to support and strengthen in the midst of life's struggles. And in certain ministry positions, being married becomes highly necessary and a potential requirement, i.e., marriage ministry. But in highlighting marriage as something that is exalted above singleness, we falsely place a label of problem where God has intended to place a label of potential.

There are two examples of single people in ministry who I would like to highlight, both being icons of the New Testament and not surprising ones at all—Jesus and Paul. And with these two examples, we are shown truths that have simply been forgotten.

The Paul who wrote the majority of the New Testament and the Paul who deeply knew ministry was also the Paul who was single.

Jesus was in relationship with God.
Jesus had a purpose.
Jesus's singleness did not hold back either one.

In discussing the singleness of both Jesus and Paul, it may be hard to see them as being "single." In our minds, I believe they have outgrown the effects of singleness that we have commonly applied to the single people we meet. But both Jesus and Paul were just as "single" as the person who you walk by every Sunday on the way to your regularly attended church seat. In dealing with the topic of singleness, our viewpoint may try to see the people who are single through either a lens of potential or problem. But just as we view Jesus and Paul with their purpose at the forefront, we need to remember to try and see others through this same lens of purpose.

Potential Lane Change Ahead

Even with two of the most prominent figures in the New Testament being single, singleness is still treated in the church with unease and hesitation. There is an underlying message that has influenced the narrative on singleness within the church. One that keeps a person from reaching their full potential until they exchange vows. With those who are single simply waiting for their season to be over. This view may not be said in words, but there is a murmur of this belief that has found itself resonating through the crowds.

The only aim in helping people should be one to encourage and equip all who find themselves within the church. Helping people to trust God that He will lead where He intends, whether it be while in singleness or marriage. And for those who are single and seeking marriage, I want to speak about the elephant-sized question in the room: does God want me to get married?

I believe that God has the best plans for each and every person, yet we simply do not understand what shape those plans may take. We can only speculate and make logical assumptions, but we must be careful to leave room for God to work out the plans He has for us, as He intends, and avoid getting hung up on what we may think they should or should not be.

I write this with the hope that the seeking of a spouse would never stop the seeking of God's will. God is a jealous God, and His plans do not include what will eventually lead us away from Him. And if the pursuit of a relationship grows to become a higher priority in a person's life than the plans God has, then the provision takes place over the provider Himself.

I believe that in the periods of waiting, whether it is in a time of waiting for the season of singleness to change or in waiting for God to bring direction, healing, or restoration, God is often testing us. Presenting us with a test to see our response to circumstances that often lack a clear direction or path to take. In this waiting time, a person's response shows where a person has placed their trust, and this also gives them another opportunity to choose where to place it. Will they wait for Moses to come down from the mountain with instructions from God himself? Or will they take what is in their own hands and build a satisfying and shiny golden calf?

If in our hearts we feel that a life of singleness is not capable of being a blessed or fulfilled life. Then this is not an issue concerning relationships, but rather an issue of how we view a relationship status and if we believe that God can truly have the best plan for a person despite a specific status.

The difference between marriage and singleness is not in the reaching of a different destination but only in the traveling of a different lane. This lane change means a person may no longer be where they were, but they are still headed in the same direction. A person's direction should always be the same, no matter a person's relationship status.

The person who truly desires a relationship must remember that God is not looking to withhold blessings. But often, the preparation required for the great things that God has planned for them is mistaken for the withholding of those very things from them. This potential conflict of trusting God for the best in the middle of the hardest moments can add to the already difficult nature of bringing the toughest questions to God for answers. But we must be careful to see that there are times when God must get us past what we hope for to get us to what He has destined us for.

In both singleness and marriage, a person will need to find and continue to find who God has called them to be, what He has called them to do, and why He loves them so much to have both for them. Neither relationship lane equips or excludes a person from this calling. Marriage is not the great commission, and singleness is not the great rejection.

Traveling on the path that God has prepared is surely a journey with many twists, turns, and lane changes, but the true destination must always be remembered. If the handling of singleness or marriage hinders the pursuit of a deeper relationship with God, then only God can redirect our path and align it with His once again. We simply must be willing to change our direction when we find that we are no longer aligned with Him.

3

The Reminder:

Marriage Is Not Superior to Singleness

From top 10 lists to the best and worst of all time, as humans we love to rank, categorize, and choose sides. Yet, we should know by now that this is not the approach to take when talking about important topics. This approach does not lead toward peace and unity—the two things that must be present in the body of Christ here on earth.

Now, if those in the church were polled with the question of which is better: singleness or marriage? There would likely be a landslide victory in favor of marriage, with the vote of my own desires also taking the side of the victor. But with this victory landslide, there is a wake of destruction that is left in its path. And any need for this question may be unnecessary because of the already present side effects that show us how short we have fallen in our treatment of singleness. Simply treating people who are single as unequal to the married version of themselves. This may not be the intention, but it is the result. This may be a harsh reality, but it is still a reality.

This reality finds itself most present when the preaching of marriage is placed at the top of the list, with single people only able to look up from where they sit as the odd ones out. Still with a place to sit but only with a reminder to learn while they wait. It may be hard to accept this as being true. But what is the counter-argument? Is stating a simple disclaimer for single people to still listen during a message about marriage enough to show that we care equally about both sides, or is it just enough to take on the appearance of it? In what ways do we pursue helping single people to the same lengths that we do married people? If you see the dilemma, you may then ask what should be done about it. But seeking to help single people is not a new attempt, and to address the topic of singleness is not to address something that has just been discovered.

But even so, singleness is still dealt with through ineffective methods and many difficult questions continue to go unanswered. Questions such as what is it that single people want or need? Do single people want the spotlighted attention? Should we try and help them find a spouse? Is there a need for a message about singleness with a disclaimer for married people? (That last wondering being of my own questioning.)

I don't think we need answers to these questions because I think this Q&A is what blinds us from seeing the concerning signs surrounding singleness and what they are actually pointing to—an out-of-balance relationship culture. One that edges itself toward the lines of idolizing one relationship status over another. This is far from a push for more content on singleness to be developed, but instead, a call for people to see what our method and message tell us about our relationship beliefs.

In the world of relationship subject matter, with singleness and marriage making up the bookends, there is a seesaw-like dynamic between marriage and singleness, and the dynamic finds itself firmly planted in the ground in favor of marriage. With resources regarding healthy singleness barely holding on, let alone able to balance it out.

This is a sign that singleness in the church is far from being understood and that it has been unable to raise the flag of importance high enough for people to see the need to understand it. And with this unbalanced culture finding itself effectively cutting single people off at the knees, without the reminder that marriage is not superior to singleness, single Christians are unable to be confident on the path that God has placed them on.

Sadly, many times I have seen single people who are strongly seeking God subconsciously longing for a marriage relationship more than a God relationship, myself included. With the church itself feeding into this struggle of good-intentioned desires, instead of supporting the seeking out and discovery of healthy singleness as God intends it to be found.

With the cultural stance of marriage as a destination and singleness as a season, we are classifying areas of God's will and putting things in places that we best see fit. With the final knockout blow to singleness found when marriage is placed in a spot that is just a level up from singleness. With all these pieces in place, what else is a single person to do but to follow the path that has been laid out before them? But it is along this very path where both singleness and marriage are hindered.

> **Without the reminder that marriage is not superior to singleness, single Christians are unable to be confident on the path that God has placed them on.**

The Single Reality

I am aware that singleness is often found at the bottom of the list of desired topics to discuss, while marriage is often found near the top. Marriage is simply a well-known topic with many scriptures and teachings that can give us a framework for healthy marriages. Yet, singleness, on the other hand, is a mystery, even though everyone who has ever tied the knot in marriage has experienced singleness. So, what if I told you that in discussing singleness that everyone is being helped, even married people? The discussion of singleness is a topic that is beneficial and necessary for everyone, married people included. But singleness is still seen as a topic that reaches the few instead of the many. Those who are no longer single are still reached when discussing singleness because all married people were once single.

One of the most important things that singleness can help a person to see are the things they are running from, and a married person may still be running from these things even if they have found someone to run to. It is crucial for a person to see their singleness in a healthy way, even if it is in their past. Having a healthy understanding of singleness is about seeing yourself in a healthy way. And being able to face singleness is more about being able to face yourself than to face the relationship you may be missing.

The discussion of singleness from a married person's perspective is beneficial in helping them to understand their own singleness, but also in helping them to apply what they know to the lives of their loved ones, their children, their co-workers, and every person that God may want them to reach. They may no longer feel the need to understand singleness to help walk out their own journey, but that does not mean it is not needed to help others in walking out theirs.

The "it may not apply to you right now" approach is the same approach that is taken when discussing marriage, but I have yet to see the same done for the discussion of singleness. We must remember that discussing singleness in the same seriousness as marriage is the biblical approach. The "just look around and find someone sitting next to you" approach to singleness is not usually a helpful one and in reality, only a side remark. While most people may find themselves unsure of how to even start in the discussion of singleness and respond by taking a back seat to the topic entirely.

Singleness is a topic that needs to be addressed. And it is one that the church needs to address in a healthy and biblical manner. Single people need to know what the church believes about singleness and what exactly it is they are walking through. How else can a person know unless they are taught? There are many resources for equipping those who seek a Godly marriage, yet a single person in the church is given nothing more than singleness in sight of preparation for marriage.

I understand that we are seeking to create a church culture where marriages are equipped to thrive and grow, and I thank God for this, yet what about singleness? Is believing that singleness is just something that God uses as a stepping-stone to marriage a healthy belief? Is hoping for the gap of singleness to be short enough a good strategy? Can we wait for people to reach marriage before we reach them?

With this approach, those who do not find themselves at the place in life where they think they should be, instead only find frustration and unease. This is true even for those who are younger and will eventually marry, with many people navigating the situations of singleness into their late twenties and thirties, often spending close to decades instead of years with a feeling of uncomfortable displacement in the church. The question we must ask ourselves is how long will we continue to ignore the reality of singleness before we choose to address it?

One Size Does Not Fit All

So, where do we start in addressing the reality that no one really wants to talk about singleness? And by this, I mean choosing to talk about singleness without an idea of marriage looming over its shoulder. There are numerous factors that could be used as a starting point, but I think the best place to start is with the discussion of why we teach what we teach. Why do we actually talk about what we talk about? The content that we discuss is often born out of a seen need for discussion but can only be developed from a place of knowledge and understanding on a topic; this shows us where the lack is found. To put it simply, content is created for what we understand and what we deem important. And singleness simply does not make the cut or reach the mark.

The beliefs that we have can be found not only in what is taught but also in what is not. What is our message saying to people? If content is developed out of the need for instruction and from a place of understanding, then what does the lack of content on singleness beyond seeking marriage tell us about our beliefs? Does this lack result from having more married people in the church than single people? Is it because single people do not have issues that are unique to them? Or is it because the topic of singleness is just not that important? Both married and single people need equal importance in the church for the body of Christ to grow. Though married people may outnumber single people in the church, singleness is no less important of a subject to be addressed, and this outnumbering is actually a major sign of why singleness needs to be addressed.

Single people make up 23 percent of active church attenders. Yet, between the ages of 18 to 49, single people make up 54 percent of the population.[1] This means that the church is widely missing the mark in reaching single people. The church is failing to reach single people because there simply is no desired seat at the table for them, only a weird metal folding chair placed near the kids' table. A seat that finds itself to be one of little respect or value. And if this is the only type of seat for single people in the church, then there is no wondering why it finds itself empty.

Over time, there has been no other picture of success painted for a Christian in the church than a married one. Painted by every stroke of time and each moment of focus invested into the topic of marriage, with the canvas found absent of successful strokes painted in favor of a single person. And with this, a person may only be able to find themselves in this painting if it is next to another.

By not investing in single people as individuals, we are choosing to not invest in the very people who eventually marry. We do not need to choose a side in the relationship status war but only to no longer let the war wage on. If we become aware of the reality that lost and broken single people become lost and broken married people. And that healed and purpose-filled single people become healed and purpose-filled married people. Then maybe the value in reaching single people for more than the reason of their future marriage will finally be seen.

Marriage does not fix what is already broken; it only magnifies what is already there, whether found broken or whole. If we desire to help marriages thrive, both the relationship and the individuals in them, then we must start by helping people when they are single to find purpose, passion, and what God has placed in their hearts. The approach of either helping married people or single people needs to be replaced with the approach to help all.

Single people should be thriving in the church, and this is far from a reality. There is a lack of vision for single people in the church, with the only common vision for single people focusing on becoming a better person while enduring their singleness. And it is because of this lack of vision that new vision must now be sought out. But in doing so, we must also hold fast to the truth that marriage holds no superiority over singleness and that single and married people find themselves to be no less than equals.

4

The Acknowledgment:

Singleness Is Difficult

Now that we can see that both singleness and marriage are good things by nature, with both allowing one to live for God fully and neither one being greater than the other. I would like to shift focus to the current view and state of singleness. And I would like to start by sharing a part of my own journey with singleness and a pivotal moment that helped to change my view of singleness.

If I reflect back on the teachings, books, and useful resources that I have encountered in my lifetime. There are many resources that have showed me how to grow in my relationship with God, people, and even myself. Resources that helped me to understand the importance of personal growth, the difficult nature of relationships, and the various hardships that a person can encounter. But even with many of these resources often aiming to help people who are going through tough situations by giving them a healthy and biblical perspective. I have seen the topic of singleness so easily and almost intentionally left out of the discussion.

For years I struggled with how to view my own singleness. From my late teenage years and into my early twenties, I looked at the tough things that I faced in my singleness as being a result of my young age. Thinking that my age must have been the reason why singleness was hard and that I should just get over it and grow up. As I approached and passed the years of my mid-twenties, the hard nature of singleness still followed me where I thought it wouldn't go. I then faced, even more, the questions of singleness and the constant struggle of wondering if it was actually a real and difficult situation to walk out.

Throughout those years, my singleness was always an area secluded from the rest of what I faced in life. Secluded by the frustration of not knowing what to do and the feeling of foolishness toward making my singleness out to be as hard as it was. With an additional cause of this seclusion being the only help or suggestions that I received telling me to just not worry about it and seek God, and then I would find a relationship eventually. And after years of that being of no help, I had hit a wall, and I needed more. But it was only when God showed me a new realization about singleness that I began to change how I viewed both myself and my singleness.

This turning point was found when God finally answered the question that I could not stop asking myself. The question of "how difficult is singleness actually supposed to be?" And God's answer showed me that singleness is not only hard but can be one of the hardest things to face in life. This newfound truth was the first thing that helped me to see that being single while wanting to marry is a truly difficult thing to face. And with this turning point, what I struggled with was finally allowed to be a real struggle. This truth may not have helped in directly answering many of the questions that surrounded my singleness, but it was a truth that gave me a desperately needed sigh of relief. And on the journey to this truth, God showed me that acknowledging singleness as being difficult is the first step to reaching the very people who are dealing with it.

In seeing singleness as something that can be difficult, this acted as the catalyst in shifting how I viewed walking out singleness and singleness itself. My shifting view of singleness led me to see that as a Christian in the church, my desire for a relationship and marriage was not just a pursuit only to be dealt with by trying to seek God and to pretend that I was just fine—perpetually burying the frustrations and questions in hopes that it would just go away. But instead, knowing that I no longer needed to belittle my own frustrations, I could finally face what I had always pushed to the wayside. With this, I found myself able to start giving God all the struggles that surrounded my singleness, and I could finally face the difficult reality of what had always found itself surrounding me. Because now all the questions I had been asking about singleness found an existence in my life as meaningful and important questions.

> **Acknowledging singleness as being difficult is the first step to reaching the very people who are dealing with it.**

Dealing With The Difficult

Most are aware of the desire that people have for human relationships as a whole and especially aware of the strong desire for romantic relationships that many have. And this becomes clear when we look at the success of championing marriage relationships above all other human relationships.

But even with this clearly seen, not having a marriage or potential marriage relationship is rarely discussed as being a hard thing to walk out. Or to put it another way, singleness is rarely seen as being difficult. The topic of singleness may not be explicitly stated in the Bible and addressed in a way that clearly states it as being difficult, but I believe that the statement of singleness being difficult is an echo of the truth that the Bible already shows us.

> The LORD God said, "It is not good for the man
> to be alone. I will make a helper suitable for
> him." (Genesis 2:18 NIV)

Genesis 2:18 is a verse that is commonly used for the promotion of marriage, and even I chose to use it in this way in chapter 2. The connection to marriage in this verse is an easy one to make. However, there are two sides to the story of this verse, and marriage is only half, with the other half often overlooked as one seeks to race from one side to the other—from singleness to marriage. For those who are walking in singleness, there is the reality of the "not good for man" part—the difficult part. As discussed in the last chapter, even though singleness is good in nature, there are still hardships that can surround it. Good does not equal easy, and this applies to marriage as well. In talking about Genesis 2:18 in relation to singleness, it may often be used to let a single person know that seeking marriage is a good thing but rarely used to offer the insight that a single person really needs—for them to know that what they are going through is hard.

In using this verse so strongly for the joys of marriage, we can blind ourselves to the hardships of singleness that a person can find themselves facing. Hardships that are faced in the shadows created by the light that is so brightly shined upon marriage. In discussing difficult things, there is a "list" that I have seen presented over the years. This list is used to help encourage those who are dealing with tough situations and usually including a mix of the following: job loss, divorce, temptations, anger, distant children, losing a family member, relationship struggles, etc. With the relationship struggles always summed up without the presence of singleness making the list.

Now, this is my personal experience, and I cannot help to believe that there are people who know the topic of singleness well enough and seek to help those who are facing it. Yet, I bring this to the forefront of attention to shine a light upon singleness and what is often faced only in the shadows. Shining this spotlight upon a reality that, even though most people who are single may not want to be reminded of their singleness, many would welcome the "I see what you are going through" moment. People simply want to be seen while going through tough situations. And with singleness, we must not only choose to see the difficult nature of it but also to make sure we acknowledge the ones who are walking through it.

Singled Out

The topic of singleness is an interesting one for many reasons. To name a few, it is a topic that includes everyone (at some point), but not many understand it. It seems to be simple in nature but resources on the topic number few. And it is a topic whose identity is not fused to marriage but rarely finds itself standing on its own in discussion. When singleness is discussed, it is often stereotyped and dealt with as an internal matter with personal growth as the main focus. The handling of singleness in these ways is often aimless, with the resulting takeaway for a single person being the two cents of "just keep seeking God, and one day you will find someone." This focus on what a person can "fix" and the simple hope that singleness will eventually end are both signs of how we fall so very short of meeting the reality of singleness head-on.

The start of approaching singleness in a healthy manner is no different than in other areas of life. And the approach of trying to fix is never the proper first step, even if it may seem that the classic question of "what about so and so?" is a good attempt. This good-intentioned attempt may often get a single person focused on the potentially debilitating parts of singleness and the parts that are often out of their control, i.e., finding a relationship. This focus on a "fix" can create an unpleasant dilemma if a single person finds themselves constantly presented with new potential solutions but never finding one that seems to last beyond a few passing moments.

Now, I hold nothing against helping single people in finding potential relationships, but how it is handled is what makes all the difference. If the finding of a relationship is the only focus in discussing the singleness of a person, then we are again failing miserably in trying to help those who are walking in singleness. This part must only be a small piece of the focus in helping a single person. The single person must be the priority of their own singleness, first acknowledging the person and the issue they are going through, before trying to find a solution. This needs to be done in order to avoid the harmful side effects that can be found attached to singleness. And a healthy focus on singleness allows a single person to center on what is in their control, rather than fixating on what is not.

If a single person sees that the only thing people care about is finding someone for them, then they will also focus on the same, and likely more than they should. It would seem that caring about setting up a single person must be the same as caring about the single person, but this can be far from the truth. And a sad reality is that some people care more about setting people up than the people they are setting up.

The understanding that must be present is that a person dealing with singleness desires first and foremost to not bear the full weight of their singleness alone, just as we all desire when we are experiencing hardships, loss, or disappointment. None of us want to face things alone and without help. None of us want to be singled out. But often the only support that a single person gets is the help to find someone else instead of the support they need to just be themselves. Many people desire to be seen as a person with pain instead of as a problem to be fixed. Our aim must be to strengthen before we seek to offer solutions. Showing people that we see what they are going through and reminding them that they are not alone, even as a single person.

Am I The Problem?

In continuing with how singleness is often dealt with, a default response is the search for a cause and effect, believing that if singleness exists, then there must be something causing it. In feeding this false idea, it can potentially lead to more problems in singleness than unhealthy singleness itself. Sadly, this false idea of singleness can create a frustrating cycle for single people to always be looking for what is wrong with themselves and to try and become the "right" person; this is unfair to single people. It is simply unfair to all people, and we must find ourselves hesitating to treat singleness in this way.

The support of this view toward singleness can be a result of believing in the stereotype of singleness as an immature or youthful situation. Or one pertaining to the "weird" or "quirky." But these are just that, stereotypes. And dangerous ones at that. With an increase in the average age of marriage, the growing reality of divorce—even within the church—and the various unforeseen circumstances that can lead to singleness, the stereotypes of singleness are far from the truth. And as a result, the topic of singleness must not be dealt with based on what may be believed about singleness, but rather what a person is facing while walking through it. So, if a person knows little about someone who is walking in singleness, then the discussion of that person's singleness is not where they should start.

At times, it is true that a single person may need to grow in certain areas of their life. Getting their life issues in order or just growing up before entering into a relationship. It is a reality that immaturity can be destructive to relationships. However, this is not the root of singleness, nor should it be the focus. Often, I hear individuals talk about their singleness and focus on the infamous question of "why AM I still single?" As if they need to awaken their inner Sherlock Holmes and solve the riddle before they can have a relationship.

When we fail to acknowledge that singleness can be something independent of personal issues, we force people to find their own conclusions of why they may still be single. Which usually leads a person to their own failures as the cause; enabling a culture where single people are unable to find confidence in themselves and further feeding into this false cause of singleness. And the unhealthy handling of singleness can further intensify with open-ended and lighthearted responses toward the subject. Responses such as "don't worry about it" instead of "that's tough." Or "you will find someone eventually" instead of "God's going to work it all out for good."

Caution must be taken to avoid what is intended to be helpful to instead become something that continues to equip singleness to be harmful. These harmful views that surround singleness must be seen as the problem to address, and never the people. Because if we allow single people to see themselves as the problem, then we have added another issue to the growing list that is found surrounding singleness.

You = Me = People

Any circumstance alone that a person faces is usually not an accurate indicator of the extent of what they may be facing. The impact of hardship and the level of suffering that a person experiences can only be found when you look at how it affects the person and not by looking at the circumstance itself.

Every situation that a person goes through finds itself mixed in with the complexity of the rest of what may be going on in their life. Becoming entangled with how a person views themselves and the path they have walked to get to where they are. Including all their hopes, dreams, hardships, and defeats. We must never look at just one situation that a person may be facing without seeing the person who is facing the situation and all that they may be facing in addition to it.

A better understanding of what a person may be experiencing in their singleness is only found by listening to what is happening in all areas of their life. An understanding found by listening to the areas they may be confused or frustrated about other than their singleness. Is their job draining them? Are their finances a constant struggle? Is their family distant? Are they struggling with their purpose in life?

Singleness becomes hardest to face when it is added to the top of all the other weights of life. And singleness is often the weighty straw that breaks the camel's back. Life cannot be separated into different categories and dealt with one at a time, with singleness being no exception to this.

Both single people and married people pay the same bills, work the same jobs, and enjoy the same pastimes. A single person may not have the relationship with a spouse that brings with it the need for hard work and tough decisions, but there are still plenty of these situations present in the life of a single person. Single people may deal with different situations than married people, but they still face the situations that require them to stretch and grow. Situations where they are faced with the same decision of putting others before themselves.

In a healthy marriage, there is a set of helping hands and another person to lean on. Another person to support you when you are weak. Another person to see the tears, share the pain, and walk out the struggles. Another person to simply see what you are going through. But the reality that lies hidden in the shadows of singleness is that a person is weakest when they are alone. Single people still have the presence of deep and meaningful relationships that build up and strengthen, but they are more fluid in nature and are less dependable at times. And this presence of only occasional support and encouragement finds itself to be one of the hardest things about singleness to encounter.

There is no benefit in comparing singleness and marriage in attempts to determine which one may or may not be harder than the other. But there is a need to see that single people are just people dealing with singleness. Single people deal with the difficult nature of singleness right alongside the many other hard things that a person may encounter, but all too easily finding themselves dealing with these things alone.

The root of singleness's difficult nature is not found in the lack of a relationship or the inability to find someone, but in the reality that life is hardest when faced alone. In desiring to genuinely care for single people, we must remind them that they are more important than their relationship status, and that the things they face do not need to be faced alone. Start by acknowledging their singleness. Start by acknowledging them.

5

The Realization:

Singleness Does Not Define a Person

Singleness. What does it say about a person? If I were to ask various people the question of what being single may tell about a person the responses would likely be mixed. The answers varying based on each individual's experience with singleness, both in their life and in the lives of those around them. Some may say it holds no weight on the scale of how to view a person. Others may say that it screams bloody murder that something must certainly be wrong. And if we observe how singleness is treated, it tends to be a weighty characteristic in how a person is viewed.

The easiest tendency is to view singleness as a possible warning sign. A red flag signaling the presence of a deeper issue in the life of a person, with this hidden issue most certainly being the thing that is stopping them from having a relationship.

The question of "there must be something wrong with them?" is often given life as a person holds on to this intriguing question of why a person may be single. And even if a person seems "normal" in every area, then a conclusion of them simply being "bad" at relationships is found lingering around the last speculative corner. But as shocking as it may be, singleness is not the all-telling sign of who a person may or may not be. It is not something found attached to a person's identity, and this holds true for a person with the status of married as well. If a relationship is at the center of the person's identity, then it is acting as an unhealthy definition. Healthy relationships do not take the role of defining people, and if a relationship does, then this is a dangerous relationship direction to head in.

A relationship status should never be at the center of how we see the identity of an individual. If this is the case, then we have lost sight of the person. And people are the only true center of a relationship or even the lack of one. If we hold the presence or absence of a human relationship to be a vital piece of a person, then what happens when a spouse passes away? Has the person lost more than a relationship? Are they no longer whole? Do they now walk through life as a lesser version of themselves? Or on the other side, what happens when a single person gets married? Are they now complete or validated as a person? Has marriage now elevated them to another level? In Genesis 2:24, we see the Bible talking about two people becoming united as one:

> This explains why a man leaves his father and
> mother and is joined to his wife, and the two
> are united into one. (Genesis 2:24 NLT)

Now, in a marriage relationship, there is the potential for a remarkable depth of connection, but this does not mean that either person has lost their individual identity. Rather, in a healthy marriage, what is given up is an individual's grasp on their personal desires and what is often desired out of selfishness. The right to a person's own decision and the seeking of what they desire are laid down for the benefit of two. And without these laid down in the presence of a marriage relationship, the relationship is found stalled on its path toward growing into what God intends it to become.

At the core of marriage is a sacred choice. A covenant decision to sacrifice one's own desires for the greater pursuit of "two becoming one." Where an individual's self is still wholly present yet no longer given priority or a place within the spotlight. Relationships can hold the greatest of meanings in a person's life, but as Christians, these relationships do not hold our definition or identity. Only our relationship with Christ can hold this kind of weight in our lives. Only in a relationship with Christ can we find our true definition and identity.

The status of being single, by nature, is not in the sole control of a person. And in treating it as a part of who they are, as a part of their identity, we only add chains to a burden that is often found to be a heavier weight than a person can bear. The realization that singleness is not the defining characteristic of a person is necessary to allow a person to be wholly themselves despite their relationship status. But if a spotlight is found shining too brightly upon a person's singleness, a spotlight which a person often cannot escape by their own efforts, then singleness can quickly become something undesirably attached to the very appearance of who they are.

> The realization that singleness is not the defining characteristic of a person is necessary to allow a person to be wholly themselves despite their relationship status.

The Person Behind The Singleness

Some may find that single people tend to avoid talking about their singleness. But what else can be expected? The way in which people talk about singleness is far from desired, and singleness is not a topic people want to focus on, simply because singleness is rarely viewed as a positive thing. And too often, it is the main event of a conversation for single people. With it being a topic of discussion that they are likely beyond tired of talking about.

If you know a person who is single and you have a desire to better understand them and what they are going through, then again, I encourage you to start with a different area of discussion. Find the areas that do not focus on their singleness but instead on them as a person. This will end up telling you more about their singleness than you think. If you do not take this step to care about them as a person before caring for them as a single person, you will soon discover the conversations will stutter and stall, not helping in growing closer to them, but over time, only pushing both sides apart. With this also holding true for conversations not related to singleness as well.

For example, most would hesitate to solely talk about the topic of finances if they knew a friend was dealing with a difficult financial situation. Instead, a person would, hopefully, bring up the topic if it seemed to be an appropriate part of their life to discuss, instead of making it the go-to conversation piece at first sight of them.

People want to be known for who they are, not solely for the things that happen around them. This is a healthy way to see people. This is the way Jesus sees us. Single or married, a person wants to be known as a person rather than a situation. An individual rather than a relationship status. Relationships must be seen as a part of a person's life rather than a part of who they are. There is always a person to be seen behind a relationship status, and this is something that is too often forgotten.

Singleness in Proper Focus

With the need to change the perspective on how singleness is viewed, it must be seen as an important area in the life of a person but only as a piece of it. Even if a person truly desires a relationship and marriage, the topic of relationships must always be found in proper balance with the rest of their life.

Take a moment to remember that you are likely not the only one who sees them as a "single person." You are one of the many that may be reminding them about this area in their life. An area that can too easily become a hyper-focused one, and likely one that a single person reminds themselves about more than anyone else. There are many non-relationship areas in life that play an important role, and relationships should not make up the sum of a person's thoughts. And if relationships find themselves taking this place in a person's life, then there should be a strong encouragement to start putting relationships within the proper perspective.

The focus on who a person is rather than a person's singleness allows you to see the person at the center of the singleness. And having this in proper focus is also important in helping single people to avoid seeing their singleness at the center of their own life. I would hesitate to sum up and treat an individual based on a single circumstance in life. In doing so, one would miss out on the whole puzzle for the sake of a few pieces.

From Hurtful to Helpful

If singleness should not be attached to the identity of a person or play a centerpiece role in one's life, then what part should it play? Is it something to just ignore? How does someone look past it and still see the person?

People tend to see a person who is single and immediately look at their singleness as an opportunity to try and plug a person into their life—problem solved. This reaction to singleness must be avoided. Even if this may seem to work from time to time, it is not the approach I would recommend. If you want to try this approach and "set" someone up. Don't just suggest but show up. If you genuinely care enough about a person to try and help them find someone as significant as their future spouse, then you should most certainly care about the rest of their life. And most importantly, how another person may end up fitting with those areas.

If all you know about a person is their name and their solo relationship status, then you are missing the necessary pieces in being able to help them to find a spouse, and this is a position that may do more harm than the intended good. Potentially leading to that person having no future desire to be "set up." With this said, I encourage the support of helping single people, and I am not against the setting up of single people, but it must be done in true support of the person. With this probably looking less like setting up a person at times and more like simply supporting them.

Now, the situation of every single person is drastically different and each person faces different circumstances, so I find it hard to write plainly about how to help single people in finding a potential relationship, as there are just too many different factors. But since I have had people ask me in the past about what they can do to help the single people they know, I would like to try and be of some practical help. I have included a section at the end of the book with some, hopefully, helpful and useful tips for those who desire to help single people.

I know that most people have good intentions, even if it may result in a failed attempt at a setup. And I want to avoid discouraging those who are seeking to help. But first and foremost, the person in the singleness must always be priority. And if this step is skipped, it is quite possible to become a thorn in the side of an already wounded individual, and in seeking to help, one only adds to the already present harm.

6

The Understanding:

Singleness ≠ Broken

When a person looks at someone who is single, especially as they get older, they may wonder why they are still single. And most often, the internalization of this question starts to create a list of potential reasons why, with the negative ones most commonly making the list. I know this to be true because, even as I write these words as a single person, I have often given voice to the all too popular lie that corners singleness: because I am single, it must mean that I am broken.

Singleness is not a disease or a sign that points toward something that is catastrophically broken. Because relationships and marriage are not a sign indicating people are healthy and whole. A relationship or the title of married does not heal or fix that which people may think is broken in single people. While it may be true that there are single people who have issues that may stop them from being in a relationship, there are just as many people facing the same issues with a person by their side and a ring on their finger.

A potential reason why there may be a "validation" of those who are married could be a result of seeing another person vouching for them as an individual—a validation of approval by another person's decision of saying "yes" or "I do." But if we take this stance and look down on singleness and single individuals because of this lack of validation, then we are choosing to place a human's opinion before God's. For God vouched for us at our worst while we were still sinners. And He validates our worth and identity as individuals, whether in singleness or marriage.

Regardless of a relationship status, we all need to be healed and made whole. To think that a relationship status in and of itself can be the telltale sign of the state of a person is strictly false. And alongside this false belief, there is the sad reality that the lie of singleness meaning "broken" is an additional cause in the breaking of single people. The understanding that singleness does not mean less than or broken helps us to align with how God views both singleness and single people.

As the body of Christ, we need to make sure we are not the ones preaching this toxic message and further allowing it to live a hidden life, often fed from our own actions. If a person believes they are broken because of their singleness, and they are unable to find a relationship to "fix" themselves, then the weight of this frustration can grow and eventually lead to further breaking them down. And with this false weight upon their shoulders, unless a person is aware of how God sees them and what He says about them. This can lead to what was once only a lie now becoming the truth. If we choose to believe the idea of any individual being less than another because of a status, then we are not choosing to see people as God does. Instead, only choosing to see them so easily as the world does.

> **The understanding that singleness does not mean less than or broken helps us to align with how God views both singleness and single people.**

Close . . . But Not Close Enough

If we are unable to see singleness through a healthy lens, it steers us toward a view that what God intended for good is not only far from good but also inferior. With an unhealthy view seeing the status of "single" as the very thing that is stopping a person from potentially reaching the mark.

Even if you would say that you don't believe in the idea that single people are broken or fall just short of measuring up. You may still unknowingly believe this about singleness. If you are no longer single and you want to test yourself on what you may believe about singleness, then ask yourself the question of what would happen if you were suddenly single? Would anything change about how you think about yourself? Would you be worried that it could change what people think of you? Would there suddenly be a newfound insecurity? These answers will show you what you believe about singleness and also reveal what you unknowingly think about single people.

Relationships are indeed an avenue in which a person can grow and continue to mature in life. However, the presence or absence of a relationship does not directly determine the level of wisdom, understanding, or maturity that a person may hold. Rather, it is the response to all the circumstances that are faced in life that determine this growth, and no one is able to avoid the ups, downs, and difficult lessons along the way that allow us to achieve this growth. Many powerful lessons are taught through marriage, but we must not forget that God is the master teacher in instructing lessons where one would least expect them to be learned.

I can personally attest that I have learned a significant amount through my experience of walking in singleness. Not because of my state of being single, but because God has used it to strengthen me in ways I did not know I needed to be strong and taught me lessons that I was not looking to learn.

Through singleness, God has taught me an abundance not only about singleness but also about many other things. Those things including trusting Him, walking in faith, the emptiness of seeking earthly desires, the perspective of His will versus my own, and even how to keep marriage in proper perspective—yes, I said marriage. We must remember that learning about marriage is not only found through a relationship with another but also through our relationship with God. He is the creator of marriage, with one of His purposes for marriage to show us more of what is found in His heart that is not found within our own. And the importance of these lessons is to learn what He seeks to teach us about His heart. With this, we must remember that the important factor in determining if a person matures and grows into a better version of themselves is not dependent on their relationship status, but rather on their own willingness to learn and grow when faced with what God is teaching them. If we lower the potential of a single person because of their singleness, then we have lost sight of the truth that our potential is found in what God has planned for us and not in our own plans or the plans of other people.

Questioned Qualifications

I want to discuss an underlying perspective about singleness that holds a view of single individuals as not quite understanding things on the level that married people might, especially pertaining to relationships. This may seem logical at the surface, but let's dive into scripture in search of some examples.

> [9] "I have loved you even as the Father has loved me. Remain in my love. [10] When you obey my commandments, you remain in my love, just as I obey my Father's commandments and remain in his love. [11] I have told you these things so that you will be filled with my joy. Yes, your joy will overflow! [12] This is my commandment: Love each other in the same way I have loved you. [13] There is no greater love than to lay down one's life for one's friends."
> (John 15:9-13 NLT)

⁴ Love is patient and kind. Love is not jealous or
boastful or proud ⁵ or rude. It does not demand
its own way. It is not irritable, and it keeps no
record of being wronged. ⁶ It does not rejoice
about injustice but rejoices whenever the truth
wins out. ⁷ Love never gives up, never loses
faith, is always hopeful, and endures through
every circumstance....¹³ Three things will last
forever—faith, hope, and love—and the greatest
of these is love.
(1 Corinthians 13:4-7,13 NLT)

These scriptures capture the words of two men, the first
scripture captures the words of Jesus, and the second capturing
the words of the Apostle Paul. With both of these writings
coming from individuals who identified with the relationship
status of single.

Now, if Paul or Jesus were single individuals in the church
today, would people listen to them? How far would they get
into these teachings before we questioned their authority on
the topic of love and relationships? Or possibly any topic they
happen to discuss for that matter.

How much could Paul possibly know about how to love if
he was walking in singleness? We know that he was well
equipped as a teacher, but without a relationship, he must have
been limited on the topic, right? Now, with Jesus being fully
God, there is a much stronger case that we would listen, but we
must not forget that He was also fully human. He learned and
grew in relationship with God just as we do. Jesus was clear in
showing us that what He taught came directly from His

relationship with God the Father, the same relationship every human has access to.

> "for everything that I learned from my Father I have made known to you." (John 15:15 NIV)

> "I do nothing on my own but say only what the Father taught me." (John 8:28 NLT)

With these reminders, Jesus showed us that it is through a relationship with God that a person develops knowledge, understanding, and wisdom, including in the area of relationships. And the most worthwhile and lasting lessons to pursue, learn, and share are the ones filled with the heart of the Father. With these lessons only learned when one finds themselves close to the heart of God. It may be through a person's experiences that God continues to equip, but only the lessons that come from God Himself carry the life that He has called us to share with others.

Wisdom For All

Now, in discussing the ability to have a deeper understanding and knowledge about relationships, there may be areas where a single person may not be able to speak directly into the heart of a situation because of a lack of personal experience. But this does not hold true for many relationship discussions, for singleness does not equal a complete lack of relationship experience as some may be inclined to believe.

Singleness does not find itself limiting a person's potential for relationship knowledge and understanding. Many single people have an in-depth understanding of relationships based on various relationship experiences throughout their life. Learning from both what they did well and what they knowingly could have handled better. For singleness does not equal only ever living alone and enjoying unlimited freedoms with no responsibility. Single people still find themselves having to share living spaces, including the always occupied bathroom. They also face the reality of coming through in their responsibilities where others depend on them. And they are certainly unable to avoid the unwanted disagreements and conversations that accompany the presence of any close relationship. In singleness, a person may not find themselves living with a spouse, but they still find themselves with relationships just the same. Relationships where people depend on them to come through, provide support, and require them to be there in moments of need.

In looking at a single person, you will find they are just as equipped to mature in Christ and seek God in the same way as a married person. They may not be facing the same exact parts of life, but they are still facing life. It should be no surprise that single people have relationships and, in some cases, more relationships than a married person. Without a spouse, there is an opportunity and need to find a similar depth of relationship in community. Even though the type of relationships may differ between singleness and marriage, it does not mean that the lessons that are learned are any different. In an individual's journey, if a person has learned what has been taught, then they have the same potential for relationship wisdom as a married person. Wisdom is calling out to all, not just the married. And with God surely teaching all, the lesson He is teaching some may very well be a surprising one. You may even find that the last person you would expect may share the very thing you need to hear. Let us not disqualify those who God may be using to speak through, including those who may identify with singleness. For God will use what seems foolish or unlikely to us to speak wisdom to the very foolishness that resides in us.

Wisdom shouts in the streets. She cries out in
the public square. (Proverbs 1:20 NLT)

For the LORD grants wisdom! From his mouth
come knowledge and understanding.
(Proverbs 2:6 NLT)

7

The Error:

Singleness as a Season

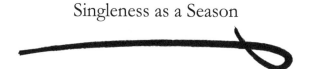

I want to start this chapter off with the statement that singleness is not a season. Yet, even as I write that statement, I also believe that singleness is a season for many. My intention in saying that singleness is not a season is to strip the "season of singleness" of its crippling frustrations—the often-added frustrations single Christians find themselves carrying as they walk with God.

In starting to talk about why singleness shouldn't be seen as a season, I would like to address singleness in regard to those who do not seek to marry. With a seasonal approach toward singleness, we can ignorantly and insensitively place a chosen lifestyle into a temporary category. With this approach, we position ourselves to only see what is missing instead of what may be found. And the life of a single person and their entire story can become overshadowed by the status of "single" alone.

We must be aware of the harm that can be done by choosing to hold on to common stereotyped stances on singleness instead of to the situational view of a person. Singleness is commonly a season, but common does not equal better than or for everyone. And again, let us not fail to see the people we so quickly classify because of a circumstance—if it be in undesired singleness while trusting God for a relationship or in chosen singleness lived in Godly contentment. And with this reminder, let us move to the discussion of the notorious season of singleness.

The most common thing that is found when we look at people who are seeking out a relationship and potential marriage is that the length of the "season of singleness" can vary greatly from person to person. And while a person walks this path out, people may recommend the popular stops of finding yourself, personal growth, seeking after God, and simply enjoying life as a single person, with these being worthwhile attractions along the way. Yet, if the perspective on these stops goes unchecked, it can create a harmful path for a person to continue to walk out. A path where a person may find themselves confused in the waiting but still told to continue seeking. Eventually finding themselves a worn-out regular at each one of these stops along this seasonal tour.

Another way that singleness finds itself being dealt with is by looking at the situations and issues of singleness as linked to singleness itself. While in actuality, singleness is just a display used to show us what is found at a much deeper level than the surface of a relationship status. And in choosing to treat it only by what is seen on the surface, we miss out on the things that actually need to be addressed. For the issues that are faced in singleness are also faced in a relationship. Presenting themselves in situations where a person must face loneliness and anxiety, desires longed for but not fulfilled, trusting God's plan when it is hardest, and questioning when and if God will ever move. These things, along with many others, must eventually be faced. And if we treat singleness as a season, then we are leaving issues untreated for another season and possibly many more.

If something is not handled in the present circumstance of a person's life, then it will surely follow them to the next. The root of many issues people face are not because of a season, even though this may be the conclusion, but most often because of being human. If we choose to view what is faced in the season of singleness as only issues of singleness, then we miss out on what is needed for singleness to become a worthwhile and beneficial season, with a person viewing what is faced in their singleness as an issue of singleness itself and not as an issue of their own. This view leads to the expectation that in the finding of a relationship, a person will also find a fix to their problems. But with the presence of a new relationship, a person soon finds that their singleness is no longer to be found, but their problems are still in their life right where they left them.

In addition to missing out on addressing underlying issues, what may be found to be more detrimental with treating singleness as a season is the creation of a cycle of questioning God's will while in the waiting. The current focus on singleness as a season has provoked into existence the common and dangerous response of "when will this season end?" This question can easily infuse itself with the way a person handles their own singleness, and it can lead to an all-consuming search for an answer. A search that overtakes the response of trusting

God despite the timeline a person sees in front of them. This leads to a person missing out on both what God wants to do in the current season of their life and what God may want to do in the next season of their life.

This ever-consuming search can be a sign of withheld trust. Trust withheld in an area where a person struggles to see God in the middle of their circumstance because they see it only as something without a purpose and that just needs to end. And the error of treating singleness as a "season" can create an expectation of God to bring rather than God to be. This unbalanced view of a season, again, can hinder what God intends the season to be. God does not waste a single moment or day in our life. And if we choose to trust God despite the outlook of the season that He is bringing us through, then we will see that He is always moving, even in the times that break us down and single us out.

> **The error of treating singleness as a "season" can create an expectation of God to bring rather than God to be.**

If Seasonal Then Side Effects

I would like to offer up a different perspective on how to see the seasonal aspect of singleness and to present some steps that can be taken to build up those who are walking in singleness. Now, I have often seen singleness treated as a season, with the potential turning point being a simple one of looking around for another single person sitting in a nearby church seat. Simple, right? If found, problem solved. Another recommendation that I have seen for single people while searching for a relationship is the presentation of a formula. One that says if you seek God and focus on personal growth, then you will be on your way to finding a relationship. Now, it is not harmful to encourage single people to walk with God and to focus on personal growth while they wait. But if we imply that as a result, eventually, they will find a relationship. Then we are creating an "if I do this, then I get that" mentality. A message that can lead a person to hear the message that they need to measure up with God before they are finally granted what they are looking for.

This If/Then mentality is the wrong connection to use in encouraging others as they seek God. Encouraging people as they walk out singleness is necessary, but it must always be followed up with the reminder that God has a plan that gives both a hope and a future, no matter the outcome of what they may be waiting for. And a focus must be put on this hope and future that God has foretold, even if it is shrouded in the unknown. Otherwise, a person will only find their focus on what is missing rather than what God is revealing. The seasonal treatment of singleness is often successful in shifting the focus off of God's intended will for a person's life toward a singular piece of it. Shifting focus toward a portion of the path and away from the purpose of the path. This greater focus on a certain part of God's will is a setup to easily wander off the path—to a place where there is little guidance or direction. This is the subtle shift toward no longer prioritizing the seeking of God Himself, but instead, something from Him that is more strongly desired.

Every person faces the uncertainty of life's circumstances and how they may or may not eventually play out. For a single person who is seeking God, there is always an uncertainty of how marriage will fit into their life. And with this uncertainty finding itself present, we should always be careful to help keep the pursuit of marriage within a proper focus. Keeping the focus centered on God while a person pursues a relationship and potential marriage.

If this focus is not kept and it finds itself shifted off of God, a person then only sees a part of God's plan and can quickly trade the unknown blessings of the future for the forcing of a potential blessing in the present. A prospective blessing seen as one that God must certainly want for them.

We know that marriage is good and from God, but we also know that singleness is no lesser of a good thing. We must be careful not to hijack what God has intended for His purpose in an attempt to better understand our situation or to help another person with their own. In not encouraging others to put their focus on God's will, but instead on only a potential piece of it, we are putting God's plans before a relationship with God Himself.

I urge everyone to reflect upon the ways in which those who are walking in singleness are being encouraged. We must always point to God as the only direction in which a person must travel. If there is any other way in which we point, then we ourselves have lost our way.

The Dangerous Fine Print

Now, let us dive a bit deeper into spelling out possible dangers that may be present while seeking a relationship and future spouse. I do not question God's intentions in how or when He chooses to bless someone with a spouse. His intentions are always good, even when it seems otherwise. The real issue is not with God and if He will or will not bless a person with a spouse but, instead, if a person has a hidden focus on finding a spouse over their relationship with God.

If this sidetracked motivation is leading a person, are they truly walking with God the way He intends? Will they be able to walk away from a promising and Godly relationship if He asks just that from them? Is their walk with God dependent on the outcome of their status of singleness changing? Is there fine print in their faith, circumstantial on if God comes through or not? This hidden outcome that a person's faith can find itself depending on is the most dangerous thing for a person's walk with God. With it not only potentially being found in singleness but in any area of life.

We see Jesus address this very situation in the life of the rich young ruler in Mark 10:17. The condition in the rich young ruler's life that stopped him from following Jesus was the inability to give up his riches to follow Jesus. And I do not believe his riches were the issue, but instead his struggle between the pursuit of God and the pursuit of what he wanted.

The danger that can be found along any path that a person travels is when there is the desire for something that outweighs the desire for seeking God. This can be true whether in the pursuit of money and fame or in the pursuit of something

"Godly," such as marriage. Yet, even though these two types of pursuits may seem different on the surface, they both hold the same potential for distancing a person from God. And I believe that for many single people, a similar condition that must be met is to find their status of "single" changed to "married."

This condition, often hidden and held deep down within, also holds onto a belief that if God does not show up as expected, then just maybe He can't be trusted. But the danger of this condition is the very reason why God is trying to remove it. If a person lets go of this, then God is able to teach the most valuable lesson. The lesson that our trust in Him should be based on nothing other than who He is, and that our desires must grow out of our relationship with Him alone; otherwise, there will always be something found along our path to lead us away from Him. In Psalm 37:4, we are called to delight in the Lord, and through this, the desires of our heart will be found. But with a priority shift toward the outcome of a season or a circumstance, we easily lose sight of delighting in the Lord. And with this lost, it should be of no mystery why we soon lose joy in the other areas of our life. The truth of delighting in God is that it will align our own desires with the ones He has for us. And if we don't believe this to be true, then the struggle between these desires will always be present.

In walking out singleness, it must not be forgotten that God is found in the middle of every moment. He is always working, no matter the outlook on the future. And I fear that if a person finds themselves waiting for a "season" to be over, they may find themselves waiting for no reason at all. And this is why I believe that singleness is not a season to get through, but only another path among the many others walked out with God.

8

The Danger:

Treating Marriage as The Destination

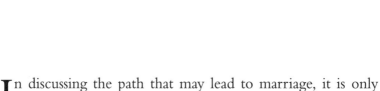

In discussing the path that may lead to marriage, it is only logical to see singleness as a step coming before marriage. It is natural to make the connection that if marriage is the ceremony of two people who were previously single, then singleness is a step that leads to it. But if there is a focus on this connection between singleness and marriage and maintaining an emphasis on singleness leading to marriage, then singleness is kept confined to only a temporary space. With the prediction of a relationship at its end and marking marriage as the destination to be reached.

The potential for danger is not found in seeing singleness coming before marriage but instead in viewing singleness with a strong focus on marriage. When the idea of singleness leading to marriage is overemphasized, we unintendedly cultivate an attitude of impatience. Watered and fed by the idea that because singleness is temporary in nature, then it must be less beneficial than marriage, and a person who is single should then be on the lookout for the end of their singleness to be within sight. And when this idea becomes fully grown, and a single person must finally confront it, they face the most difficult of questions.

Questions such as, if marriage is the destination of singleness, then why am I still single? What is stopping me from getting there? Is there something I am missing? And with these questions forming only the base upon which many other questions of doubt and discouragement can build, the questions that a single person can find themselves asking continue to pile up. What must I do to get married? What did "so and so" do to get married? Is there something wrong with me? Why, God, am I still waiting?

Walking out singleness with a temporary and less-than attitude often leaves no room for God to use singleness in the way and capacity that He intends. The short-term mentality becomes the thief that steals the patience needed to work out what God is working on, in His timing and His way. This short-term view of singleness is often connected to a hidden deadline. A deadline of expectation for God to move within a certain time frame, after a predetermined life event, or by a precise age. A deadline for God to finally end the temporary reign of singleness. If God beats the deadline and moves in time, then He has come through. And if He seemingly does not, everything soon finds itself to be questioned. But this is not how God works. For God is wise enough to follow His own timeline and never our deadlines.

If we find ourselves trusting in how we think God is working over who we believe Him to be, then we soon find ourselves putting our trust in our faulty ability to understand how God works. His ways are far beyond what we can comprehend, so we must remember to put our trust in the character of who He is over how we may see Him working in a circumstance.

If our priority is out of order, with a desire for a certain outcome replacing the desire for God's will to be done, then a constant feeling of being failed and forgotten will be found. And without the proper priority in place, a potential danger is that the treatment of marriage as the destination of singleness can hinder the pursuit of God's will if one is waiting to arrive.

The expectation of marriage as a destination reached, if gone unfulfilled, can commonly lead to moments of feeling that God is uncaring, distant, and altogether absent. If we are not on board with trusting His plan for our lives, then whose plan are we choosing to trust in? Trusting in God in all areas of our lives, singleness included, allows God to be God. This allows God to move how and when He knows best, and that is the only way we want Him to move, but recognizing this truth often only occurs after we have already placed our trust in Him.

Even if you are not the one dealing with singleness, it is important to remember to respect this path if another person is walking it out. Don't try to change the path a person is on because you think it is in their best interest. If they are seeking God and putting their trust and hope in Him as they walk out their journey, then all you need to do is to support them along the way.

This is true for every person who is single. You must have respect for both the person who does not desire to marry and for the person who does but it is yet to be seen. Because God's paths are rarely straight and surely riddled with many twists and turns. As it says in Proverbs:

> We can make our plans, but the LORD determines our steps. (Proverbs 16:9 NLT)

> **The treatment of marriage as the destination of singleness can hinder the pursuit of God's will if one is waiting to arrive.**

Detours, Distractions, and Destinations

Over the years, I have seen how God has guided me as I have walked out my faith, and in all honesty, it has often widely missed the mark of making any sense to me at all. When I try to aim for a destination, God reminds me that I need to trust Him when it feels like I am facing a detour. Because when God is leading me into what I believe to be a detour, He is actually leading me away from one.

If we determine in our minds to make marriage a destination, then we continue to miss out on the truth that the paths of both singleness and marriage are equal. Both being avenues by which God uses to shine the light of Christ and to help a person grow in maturity and in relationship with Him. And as many circumstances in life show us, it is not up to us to determine where we find ourselves walking out our faith. It is only up to us to walk out our faith wherever we find ourselves.

What God desires for our lives is to avoid getting lured away from Him by the potential distractions that we may stumble upon. These distractions are often good in nature but can quickly become what hinders the plans that God has for us. Let us guard ourselves against falling into a mindset that certain paths are any greater than or less than another. The many paths that God leads us on may carry different scenery, but they all lead us to the same intended destination. A destination of becoming more like Christ and helping others do the same.

This is our Great Commission. To first be disciples of Christ and then to go and make disciples. But with a mindset of "arriving" somewhere along God's path, it will surely cause us to stop short of getting to where God is calling us to go. We will unknowingly put markers along our path on behalf of God, soon finding ourselves conflicted between the markers we have placed and the direction that God is leading us in. Let us yield to trusting God's directions over our own, with only one destination within our sight.

The Need to Burn a Few Bridges

In revisiting what I have heard taught about singleness, singleness is always discussed in relation to marriage; again, we all see the correlation that can be made. But in doing so, we have created a gap between the two relationship statuses and have furthered the cause in distancing one status from the other. This distance then becomes a cause of confusion when we find ourselves unable to bridge the gap for the people we seek to care for.

Whether single or married, a person should be looking to grow and mature in their faith. A marriage ring is not a trophy on someone's hand, rewarded once their life is in order, but instead, marriage is meant to be a part of God's plan and not intended to replace it. God uses marriage within His plan to help imitate the sacrificial and undeserved love that God shows us. The very love we all struggle to show, whether single or married.

Marriage is not meant to be an acknowledgment of how good a person is but a relationship in which a person can be loved and accepted at their worst. Where a person is found in the middle of their imperfections and loved in no less of a way, just as God has done for us.

We must remember that marriage is not a destination in God's plan, found on the opposite side of a bridge from singleness, but only a lane change within it. Our walk with God is not intended to be seen with a handful of destinations at which we may arrive at, but instead, to see ourselves sharing steps with God Himself and with the people He puts in our life.

If we don't find ourselves sharing these steps, we can strip God of sharing a relationship with us and force Him to become only a distant director. This is where we lose our way, for it is only in true relationship with God where we find our directions. It is only in walking along the path with God where we find His will.

Single or married, a side must not be chosen. We must care for all in the body of Christ and help everyone to grow and walk closer to God. For we are all called to the same destination. But to continue to move forward, we may need to burn a few of the bridges that have been built between singleness and marriage. In order to help everyone reach the destination that God has intended: growing closer in relationship to the one who made us and showing others how to do the same. The message for strong marriages should certainly be taught and encouraged, but it must never overtake the message for people to seek the will of God and to do that in all circumstances of their life.

We must remember to care for people who are single as individuals walking out a path of singleness, instead of as only people with a label telling of their singleness. This helps to equip single people for the work God has placed in front of them. Instead of only for the potential relationship waiting for them. In doing this, there will be a confident move of single people toward God and His will for their life, and a pursuit of not just a portion or highlight of His plan but all of it.

9

The Pursuit:

Caring For People, Every Single One

Singleness is a topic that needs to be addressed for many reasons, but it only needs to be addressed because we have lost sight of what Jesus has called us to do. Even though the topic of this book can be placed in a category of relationships, the heart behind it is for people—the ones often overlooked and defined by a label. And if people are the heart behind it, then caring for and loving them is the reason why it beats. For this is what Jesus has called us to do—to love one another.

There are many more questions to ask and answers to be found regarding singleness and what has been discussed so far. But that is not where we need to start to move forward in caring for single people. So, I want to talk about what we need to focus on: caring for people. If we desire to care for and reach people effectively, we must echo in our lives what Jesus lived. He looked past all the labels, ignored every cliché category, and found the individual. How beautiful this must have been to witness. To see Jesus look wholeheartedly at a person for "who" they were and not "what" they may have looked like in the moment. This must have left countless in speechless amazement and certainly many more in great confusion.

It was always the label or condition that was brought up when the disciples or Pharisees talked about a person. For it was all they were able to see, and this is often what we choose to see. Yet, caring for a person before caring about a label is the beginning of loving as Christ loved.

If we listen to the labels screaming at us from first appearance or spoken word and let that stop us from reaching a person. If we hold people to the level of the labels that so easily attach themselves. Only viewing a person as single or married, rich or poor, same race or different. Then we have taken on the sight of man and not of Christ. Setting ourselves up to let an appearance tell a person's story and letting a label live their life for them. We never read of Jesus struggling to eat with the tax collectors, avoiding conversations with prostitutes, or taking a leper-free route. Because the first thing Jesus saw was the person and never the label.

> **Caring for a person before caring about a label is the beginning of loving as Christ loved.**

Some Labeled, But All Broken

It may be embedded in our human nature to label and put things in what may seem like the "correct" category. At times, it may help us make sense of who we encounter, what we encounter, and more about each encounter itself. But our human nature is what we are to live contrary to. It is what comes easy, yet always brings with it the desires we are called to let die. It is in living by these desires that cause us to so easily miss out on what God wants to do here on this earth.

When we talk about labels, we immediately face the first area we often apply them to—appearances. And as humans, we love appearances, but there is a long list of cliché reasons of why it is not good to judge by appearance alone. And this should not be surprising, as God Himself takes little account into the appearance of a person.

> But the LORD said to Samuel, "Don't judge by his appearance or height, for I have rejected him. The LORD doesn't see things the way you see them. People judge by outward appearance, but the LORD looks at the heart."
> (1 Samuel 16:7 NLT)

Time after time, the Bible shows us that if we look to an appearance for understanding and insight, then we will miss the very thing that God is doing. If humans were tasked to write the endings of the most famous Bible stories without knowing the end that we know, they would look quite different.

Saul would have stayed king in his palace, and David would have stayed shepherd in his field. Mary and Joseph would have quietly broken up and remained "just" friends. Jesus would have required his twelve disciples to have three to five years of ministry experience and less of a fish smell. And Paul, the persecutor of Christians, would not have made it onto the list of people to even proofread the New Testament.

We know that appearances have never been on the list of God's requirements, and we need to reassess how high on our own lists they may currently stand. The discussion of relationships in this book is a secondary topic, but it becomes primary when we fail to do what is most important: to care for and love people. If we start with people and caring for their individual needs, then all the previous chapters in this book become needless.

Jesus did not seek out to care for the lepers, the prostitutes, and tax collectors because of a label, but instead, He chose to seek out the rejected, the abused, and the outcast because of their brokenness. He sought out the ones who were broken and were unable to hide it. And it was because of their unavoidable conditions that they found that there was nothing stopping them from coming to Him.

But even though the disciples and Pharisees did not carry a label of brokenness put on by man, they were just as broken as every leper, prostitute, and tax collector that Jesus encountered. They may not have shared the same "broken" label as the people that Jesus often accepted, but they were no different. And if we choose to see only labels, then we will miss out on the truth that labels only separate, but our brokenness brings us all to the feet of Jesus.

Love Past The Label

Humans can certainly be found in every form—drastically unique appearances, different cultural backgrounds, and a vast spectrum of financial status' all tied up with the countless bows of opposing beliefs. But we must be self-aware of how our human nature is inclined to view people and instead choose to view them how Jesus did.

Jesus saw the brokenness and pain that defeated people instead of how humans defined them. He sought to bring healing to the areas that stopped people from coming closer to Him, and not just healing for the disabilities that stopped them from coming into a building. Jesus simply saw what others chose not to see, what they could not see: the heart. And we need to desperately pray for this same sight. To see people in the same way as Christ, choosing to take our eyes off the appearance that we so easily cling to and to let go of the things that help us "understand" what we see, rather than who we see.

Appearances can give us a feeling that we are able to understand the narrative of our lives and the lives of others. A narrative we often try to create in seeking to better understand God on our terms. But in doing so, we are forced to lean on our own understanding to fill in the many gaps that are quickly found in the view that we have created. This understanding makes sense to our human nature, but it finds itself based on the logical appearance of how God should work instead of how He often does work.

The command we have been given is a simple one; to love one another. Not asked to love when it makes sense or urged to love because it makes us a "good" person as a result. It is just a command to love people, which means it is not optional. And when we treat it as optional, love is quickly found in tragically short supply, leaving us wondering why the world is in such a broken state but still seeking to fix it in another way.

The reality is that where love is meant to bring those who are different together it is pushed aside, and instead, people are torn apart because of their differences. When love is supposed to lift those who are weakened, a nose is raised to a person as one looks down upon someone, only being able to see them by their own judgments. And in the moments when people are seen as "others," instead of being loved as another, the lesson is missed that there are no "others" in this world but only those who are labeled differently than ourselves. People who carry the same fears, flaws, and failures that we all do. But who may have been given a different label than our own. What will happen if we follow Jesus's example? What would that look like for single people? What would that look like for all people? These answers are not hard to find because we can see what happened when Jesus showed us.

Zacchaeus was at the back of the line, far from being accepted because of his job as a tax collector, but the first to be given a seat at the table with Jesus.

The woman at the well was isolated from others because of her reputation but not from encountering the presence of Jesus.

The lepers were cast out because of their unclean condition but handpicked for a healing touch from Jesus.

Encountering Jesus was indeed something to be witnessed. This is where people found freedom from the labels that separated them from others and where they experienced healing in the midst of their pain. Encountering Jesus was simply where "on earth as it is in heaven" happened every day and encountering each one of us should be just the same.

A Hard and Most Beautiful Truth

If we are honest, when we see a person who looks different than us, what will we find? Will we find ourselves reacting in a way that holds back loving them because they don't quite fit those we want to love? Do our thoughts get stuck on what could happen because they seem too messy to love? Or do we find it is just too inconvenient to actually love them altogether?

This is the scary reality of conditional love, and I am scared most of all for myself because I have found this to be true in my own life. I struggle to loves others with all that I have, often only loving with what I have left to comfortably spare. This type of love is still a form of loving others, but this is not what is asked of me. This is a conditional love that falls so utterly short. And this is the type of love that Paul warned Christians about.

> Don't just pretend to love others. Really love them. (Romans 12:9 NLT)

Paul warned about a love that walks, talks, and acts like a real form of love but that is not quite the genuine love we are called to. And this warning certainly still applies to us today. Paul shows us that he takes the command to truly love one another very seriously. He knew that we can be inclined to make it look like we are loving others, instead of holding fast to the command to actually love.

In the moments where I fall short of this type of love and loving like Christ, there is sadness and a loss for words. Sadness for my inability to genuinely love another person, and a loss for words as I look at the true and unconditional love that Jesus displayed on this earth. In these moments, God shows me that there is nothing that I can use of my own ability to be able to love in this unconditional way. The truth is that I will always fall short. But then God reminds me of the most beautiful of truths. I am reminded that I do not have to love from my own human capacity, but instead, I am simply called to love from the overflow of how God has loved me. And I am only able to truly love others by embracing how God has shown me love and then choosing to share this with others.

I will never be the source of God's love but only an imperfect human being choosing to carry this perfect and unconditional love to others. I will certainly fall short when trying to love others like Jesus did, but I must hold on to the command that I am called to love, no matter what. Let us carry this love to the world. Let us follow the example that Jesus lived out. Seeing past the labels, serving beyond the status', and unconditionally loving the individual. Remembering that our love for others does not come from ourselves but only from that which God has placed within us. And choosing to always love people no matter their appearance, social standing, or relationship status.

[36]"Teacher, which is the greatest commandment in the Law?"

[37] Jesus replied: " 'Love the Lord your God with all your heart and with all your soul and with all your mind.' [38]This is the first and greatest commandment. [39]And the second is like it: 'Love your neighbor as yourself.' [40]All the Law and the Prophets hang on these two commandments."
(Matthew 22:36-40 NIV)

Practical Steps:

The Setup Without The Downside

Some may ask the question of how to actually be of help to a single person who desires to marry. Seeking to help them as they look to find a potential relationship. Or in the words of some, helping to set them up.

There are no simple answers to this question because it can simply become too complicated too quickly, as most relationship situations can easily find themselves becoming. But in hopes of being helpful to those who want to try and be of help, here are some practical steps.

But first, before we move on, we must remember that it is not about finding an easy and quick-fix solution for a person. Rather, the aim must be to care about the person before the success of a setup. If this is kept as the primary focus as a person tries to lend a helping hand, then both sides will be better off no matter the outcome.

Start Here

The initial step that is rarely found when a person is trying to help a single person to find someone who they might be interested in is the step of gaining an understanding of what that person is looking for in a potential relationship. This is a vital step, as it is the step that actually leads to learning more about the single person themselves. Without this, both sides can quickly become frustrated. The single person most of all because they have found another person who is only a little bit interested in their situation and quite uninterested in them as a person. If you choose to get to know a single person without a focus on their singleness, then they will see that you are interested in more than just their relationship status. And this will go a long way. Allowing them to see that you are trying to help them, instead of just trying to help set them up.

Care Enough To Be Aware

In my opinion, the beginning of a successful setup is not to match a list of criteria or to check off a bunch of boxes, but rather to have the awareness to avoid the cringeworthy moment often found in a setup. The moment of internal bewilderment that a single person can face wondering, "Is this what they think of me?" This moment often occurs after being asked the infamous question of "What about so and so?" I would venture out to say that there are many people who have experienced this very moment in life. It is a common result from good intentions mixing with an unequipped understanding. Again, this is not a result of bad intentions but often a result of a setup missing the mark by more than just a few miles. Some setups may hit the mark in matching two people together. But if you find that you often encounter single people who are "just not interested" in being set up, this is likely a polite response in attempt of avoiding the simple answer of an emphatic *NO!* To try and avoid this response, be aware of your suggestions and don't find yourself just suggesting anyone.

No Simple Answer To Why

Another reason that many single people will say they are "just not interested" is because they know that if they reply with a "no," there is often the secondary question of "why?" This can create a difficult situation for a single person to try and navigate through on their way to an answer. It is incredibly hard to come up with an explanation of why there is a lack of interest in another person. Most single people know the real answer is lengthy and that those who are asking the question do not actually care about hearing out the real and full-length response.

The single person's real response to the question of "why" will tell you what they are actually looking for in a relationship, and again this is what should be known from the start. In caring about setting someone up, you need to care about their answer to the question "why" before you ever ask a question about "who." You must have an understanding of the type of person they have in mind before you start looking to help them find that person.

Right One Or Worn Out

The driving force behind the "setup," or helping two people to meet, should not be to just meet anyone but to meet, what I loosely call, the "right" person. Now there is rarely harm in two people meeting by means of a setup, but instead, the potential harm may result from wearing a single person down with too many bad experiences. Worn down by facing too many setups that always present people who are far from what they are looking for in a potential relationship. The potential of becoming worn out by bad setups will vary from person to person, but it is something to be aware of when seeking to help.

Now, it is impossible for a single person to know everything about a person at first glance, and a single person must be careful to avoid looking for the "perfect" person. But a healthy view, in the pursuit of meeting the right person, is one that seeks to meet someone that checks off a few of the important "potential" check-boxes. With this, the likelihood for a relationship to form greatly increases. This should be the desired aim of both the single person who is looking for a potential relationship and also for the person who is seeking to help them in their pursuit.

This can certainly become a trial and error process, but it often finds itself getting stuck in the unending cycle of being set up with the "wrong" type of person. And in labeling a person as the "wrong" type, this is not implying that a person has something wrong with them, but instead, they are not necessarily what a person may be looking for in a potential relationship.

In all of this, it must not be forgotten that just because a person desires a spouse that loves Jesus, it does not mean that they desire any spouse that loves Jesus. I hope that these insights may be of help to those who truly desire to support those who are single and seeking a relationship. And that it helps in making sure that we treat people in a way that truly supports them as people and not as a status that often seeks to define them.

Notes

Chapter 3 - The Reminder

1. Joyce Chiu, "A Single Minded Church," Barna Group, February 9, 2017, www.barna.com/single-minded-church.

About

Joshua is the founder of Living to the Utmost. He enjoys writing about life and many of its questions. He resides in Grand Rapids, MI, where you can find him working on various creative projects or learning a new hobby.

You can find more of his writing at Livingtotheutmost.com